THE
IDIOSYNCRATIC
GARDEN

How to create and enjoy a personalized outdoor space

H. Ralph Schumacher
with Elizabeth S. Schumacher

Archway Publishing books may be ordered through booksellers or by contacting:

Archway Publishing
1663 Liberty Drive
Bloomington, IN 47403
www.archwaypublishing.com
844-669-3957

ISBN: 978-1-4808-4799-6 (sc)
ISBN: 978-1-4808-4798-9 (e)

Print information available on the last page.

Archway Publishing rev. date: 11/06/2023

Contents

Foreword and Acknowledgments

My husband, Ralph, was himself a man of idiosyncratic talent (his long and illustrious career in medicine is detailed at the-rheumatologist.org/article/triple-threat-rheumatologist). He had big ideas, and he was driven to bring his ideas to fruition. It was Ralph's vision to turn the barren hillside behind our first home into the special garden it became, and it was his idea to write this book. Ralph was a prolific writer, publishing more than 400 medical research articles and an additional 200 reviews, book chapters, and editorials. When he was ready to start this book, he enlisted Jan Dinnella, his Penn Rheumatology colleague, to help him on the project. During the period in which he was writing it, he was diagnosed with the neurodegenerative disease ALS (commonly known as Lou Gehrig's disease). As ALS took more and more from him, including his ability to speak or use his arms and legs, working on this book was something he enjoyed and brought him a sense of purpose and meaning.

For many decades and with this project in mind, Ralph had documented innovative details and scenes from our garden and the many gardens we visited in the Philadelphia area and beyond. His goal was to inspire people to consider how they might create and enjoy their own idiosyncratic gardens. He had completed a first proof of the book before he unfortunately lost his life to ALS in 2017. In the days before his death, he could no longer communicate verbally, but he was able to make his wishes known with eye movements and a letter board. I promised him that I would finish the book, and thanks to the help of many wonderful people, it is finally finished! I would like to express my gratitude to my daughters, Heidi Wilson and Kaethe Schumacher, and my friend and Garden Accents manager, Madeline Duffy, for reviewing and editing the manuscript and always being there to support me; to Beverly Fitts, my gardening expert friend, for double-checking the many plant names; to Razelle Frankl for encouraging me to find publishing professionals who could help fulfill Ralph's vision; and to Diana Cobb and Nancy Rutman, the terrific pros who brought it to completion.

We hope you enjoy our labor of love and that it inspires you to see gardens in a new way.

Elizabeth S. Schumacher

Introduction

Every garden, whether small or monumental, offers opportunities for its designer to add unique, creative touches, or to be idiosyncratic. "Idiosyncratic" may seem like an unusual term for describing a garden, but the word is generally defined as "pertaining to something peculiar to an individual," with some synonyms being "distinctive," "personal," or even "quirky." Because gardens are so personal to their creators, most are, in many ways, idiosyncratic.

Let's explore some innovative ideas illustrated by my photographs of the multitude of gardens Liz and I visited over a span of more than 40 years. Most are Philadelphia-area gardens, including the treasured one we created together in Gulph Mills, Pennsylvania. Our wish is that the images and concepts on these pages will encourage new approaches for developing distinctive features for your own gardens.

H. Ralph Schumacher

1

Starting to Innovate

There can be quite a variety of reasons to begin innovating, and necessity will definitely be the mother of some of those innovations. Let's begin with examples from Liz's and my Gulph Mills garden, starting with those triggered by evolving needs. The thin strip of lawn behind our home began to be trampled by both us and visitors walking toward our brick patio. An obvious suggestion was to insert some stepping stones. We chose gray flagstone, which was the same material as in the adjacent steps. How to transition between the flagstone and brick was successfully solved by this yin-yang flagstone-and-brick platform at the bottom of the steps.

Necessity can also determine some plant placements that may actually work out well. At a nursery, we found an umbrella pine (*Sciadopitys verticillata*) that we had been coveting, but it was fairly large for us to handle, with a good-size rootball. We thought it could be a great accent on the slope of our hillside garden but had no idea how to get it up the steep incline. We finally asked our uphill neighbor to allow us to bring it down on a trolley through their yard. As we tried to lower it down the slope, we lost control, and it rolled unimpeded to the edge of the broad flat lawn. We decided that there it should remain, and today it thrives and serves as a great divider of the halves of our croquet court. With its array of umbrella-like needles, it is an important presence even in the snow and mist of winter.

Our home, which we purchased in 1967, had what we felt was a totally inappropriate straggly privet hedge along the street curb. Since I in my youth had enjoyed the satisfaction achieved by trimming my parents' hedge, I looked for a place to give it a fresh start. There was a nascent series of wood steps up the barren hillside behind the house. I decided to begin to move the privet to the border of the steps to provide definition. Over the years and with additional purchases of privet (plus lots of trimming), this has added a good touch of formality and structure. Seen just starting to leaf out in the spring (below left) or throughout the summer (below right), the hedge gives strong lines to our otherwise scattered, rather informal, and eclectic plantings and garden areas that evolved.

Travel experiences can also provide a motivation for innovation. As we traveled, we were often interested in items or ideas that would remind us of the trips and add personal touches to the garden. In eastern Europe, we had loved some of the small roadside religious shrines, and we wanted to recreate their ambience back at home. We were fortunate to find a lead St. Francis plaque and then a carpenter who could make us a redwood shrine-like stand. This is placed at the end of a lawn along a path leading up through a wooded area. There it continues to be a delight for us and for visitors as they wander the garden.

When our two daughters were young, and later when we had young grandchildren, a jungle gym, seen here in the background (below left), was a great attraction. In between children and grandchildren, it was used as a support for clematis. Now, painted purple, it is a surprisingly interesting "work of art" even throughout the winter. In the summer, it has functioned as a frame variously accented by honeysuckle, tomato plants (below right), and most recently a trumpet vine.

An experienced Swarthmore gardener has a wonderful, large garden, but one of his most innovative features suggests that he eventually ran out of space in the soil and created this succulent planting (enhanced with a draping white-flowered clematis) on the roof over the front entrance to the home. Another gardener used succulents to make a wreath to further embellish her decorative fragments of antique cast iron.

This "crystal garden" was a very functional area for rooting new plants under glass, but the variety of glass containers turned out to be so interesting that it became a highlight of the creative homeowner's landscape.

Some plants are special because of the wonderful memories they evoke. While we lived in Boston in a small apartment, we took our 1½-year-old daughter, Heidi, to the Arnold Arboretum for an outing. Despite having no experience yet with horticulture, we were struck by the lovely heart-shaped leaves of a certain tree and held Heidi on a low branch for a photo. When we moved to Pennsylvania, we were looking for a tree to provide some shade near the house. We recalled that arboretum excursion and checked the photo we had taken of Heidi. For some unclear reason, we had recorded the name of the tree, katsura (*Cercidiphyllum japonicum*), and quickly decided that buying one would be a great reminder of our time in Boston. Years later, this beautiful multistemmed specimen shades the patio beside our home.

Why waste the space under your barbecue? I wonder how often this barbecue is used, or whether we should credit it as a pretty innovative modern sculpture.

Opportunities from Your Terrain

Don't be daunted by an apparently difficult terrain. A hillside may give you a perfect place to do something especially interesting and distinctive. Here a pond surrounded by plantings is a delightful discovery only after scaling the slope behind this home (below left). A wooded hill behind a home (below right) allowed for the carving out of paths leading to a series of special areas. A much more formal (and not inexpensive) approach to taming a slope is this stone and planted descent to a swimming pool just out of view in the bottom photo.

Might a variation on one of these styles work for you? In an example from our own generally informal hillside, strong lines are introduced by the carefully trimmed privet hedge lining the steps. The hedge also helps define a number of distinctive garden rooms, one of which features dwarf evergreens (below left). Creating transitions between levels offers the chance for innovative choices such as this millstone step used in a Philadelphia garden (below center). A beautiful array of evergreens (below right) can be enjoyed by climbing the bank from which you can also see the neighbors' home and "borrowed landscape."

Plantings along garden paths are always a pleasure, but note how this assortment of hostas can be even better appreciated when seen along a slope (below left). A descent to the lawn behind the home of this Unionville horticulturist is lined with stone steps that have been softened by interspersed low plantings (below right).

Hollows or depressions on your property can also present both challenges and opportunities. These two gardeners used their low areas perfectly as sites for ponds and a pool. Less close to the home might you develop a bog garden in a hollow?

What can you do with a flat property? Really level ground poses the challenge of breaking up the flatness and creating areas of interest. Elevated beds (below left) accomplish this with plantings of varying heights and introduce a practical assortment of herbs for the kitchen. An attractive fence and gate in a Devon garden (below right) breaks up a flat area and creates a hidden spot on the other side to be explored.

This more modest fence, pictured directly below, breaks up a long backyard garden in a similar but subtler way. Walls can also divide flat areas and provide structure for separate garden rooms, such as the space defined by a low wall in the foreground and a tall wall at the rear (bottom left). The wall in this Chestnut Hill garden (bottom right) is used as a background for attractive plantings and to create a distinct area for a bonsai collection.

A decorative handcrafted arch, like this beauty by Greg Leavitt, is another way to segment a level area and transition between garden spaces.

3

Using Plant Collections

Over the years special interests may change, but always keep an open mind about making space for evolving new interests. The following are two examples of collections from our own experience. You can be really idiosyncratic by focusing on massing the plants you collect in a virtual monoculture of bed after bed of a certain species as you might see in a nursery. How about instead trying to integrate your collections seamlessly among other plantings? By making sure you can see these plants throughout the year, you will be able to enjoy some of the interesting subtleties that deserve your attention.

Rhododendrons and Azaleas

As our own garden evolved, we were drawn into a local chapter of the American Rhododendron Society by enthusiastic friends and by the glorious displays of azalea and rhododendron flowers on our property each spring. Soon we had files on more than 75 plants and enjoyed noting at what time each flowered, which were doing well at which sites, and more growing details. Rhododendrons and azaleas are best integrated at the edge of woodlands (below left) and in combination with other acid-loving plants such as enkianthus and mountain laurel. One example of a successful combination we enjoyed was this white azalea with the appealing new red growth of a pieris (below right). We used the small, white-flowering rhododendron 'Balta' immediately adjacent to our glass plant room (above). This

looked great for a year but then taught us that most rhododendrons do not continue to do well in the more alkaline soil next to a home's foundation.

We found other personal pleasures from our collecting when we occasionally won a prize at the yearly Rhododendron Society truss shows. This cross, *Rhododendron* 'Mars' x *yakushimanum*, was a prizewinning example.

You can add to your pleasure by extending the flowering season of some of the plants you are collecting by choosing both early and late bloomers. For example, hybrids of *Rhododendron nakaharae* still have profuse flowers in late June. These wonderful low-growing, June- and July-blooming azaleas, pictured here bordering a front walkway (below left), also remind us of Taiwan, where Liz lived for four years while she was in high school and where our family spent six months in 1989 while I was on sabbatical from the University of Pennsylvania. *R. nakaharae* azaleas are native to the mountainous areas of Taiwan and were originally cultivated there by a Japanese horticulturist during the long Japanese occupation that finally ended after World War II. *R. maximum* (below right) also boasts very late blooms, as shown in this early-July view.

Most of the year, the foliage is what you see, so another interesting twist on the collection can be to seek out unusual leaves or plant habits. Yakushimanum rhododendrons, such as the specimen at left, feature fuzzy indumentum and dramatic powdery white new growth, making them obvious targets. *R.* 'Neat-O' (right) has an attractive cinnamon-colored "dusting" of indumentum in summer.

Foliage shapes can vary from the extremely narrow leaves of *R. stenopetalum* 'Linearifolium' (below left) to the subtly rounded ones of *R.* 'Bow Bells' (below right), seen here after a summer shower.

A friend showed us this unusual curled-leaf variety, *R. maximum* 'Curly Leaf'.

Because most rhododendrons are evergreen, they contribute rich color to the winter garden. This is true except when the temperature falls to about 0 degrees Fahrenheit. Their dramatic, protective tight curling in severe cold (below left) is interesting if not especially attractive. Collections can give the opportunities for some unusual detours! I was briefly interested in utilizing electron microscopy, which I used in my medical research, to try to explore the mechanisms for the curling. I wanted to get images of both normal and curled leaves but got only images of normals (below right) before wisely deciding that it was hard to justify the use of research grant funds for this.

 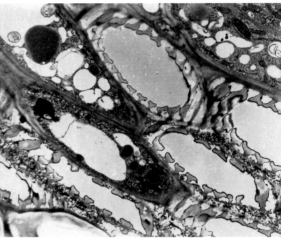

The curling is clearly temperature related. Even when the plant is coated with snow and ice, you can still see nice, minimally uncurled leaves when the temperature is not as low.

An alert idiosyncratic rhododendron collector can get some unusual fall views like the apparently whiskered specimen below, which has been bedecked by needles from an overhead pine. A few rhododendrons, such as a PJM Group hybrid (center) and *R. schlippenbachii* (bottom), will produce sporadic fall color.

Those Versatile Viburnums

We love viburnums, which include some small trees and many bushes with dramatic sweeping shapes and virtually year-round interest. With meticulous pruning and removal of water sprouts, Liz, with year-after-year persistence, has shaped a glorious, attention-getting *Viburnum sieboldii* from a scraggly specimen we found adjacent to the garage when we moved into our home. Below, we see the shape and May flowers.

As the spring flowers of *V. sieboldii* fade, berry-like drupes begin forming on showy red stems (below left) and persist into winter. The knobby bark (below right) remains attractive even after the plant loses its leaves.

The bare stems of this versatile woody plant let us see the nest of our yearly resident birds and also look perfect with a decoration of light snow. It's a true four-season standout.

On the other side of the garage is another viburnum we enjoy as we come and go in all seasons, a leatherleaf viburnum (*V. rhytidophyllum*). It has interesting fuzzy new growth, corrugated green foliage, and classical flowers that evolve from bright white to yellow.

The horizontal branches of the doublefile viburnum *V. plicatum* f. *tomentosum* 'Mariesii' (left) can be used to create a floral canopy over a stone sculpture.

Our linden viburnum (*V. dilatatum*), pictured below, boasts great fall color as well as the berries that are such an attraction with many viburnums. In some locations, however, the shrub is considered invasive.

The linden viburnum's berries have persisted long enough to contrast with an early-December snow on a bank visible from our kitchen. One year, the beautiful red berries of tea viburnum (*V. setigerum*), shown below right, lasted until February.

Collectors are always looking for new ideas. Here, on a December visit to the Morris Arboretum, I was checking out a variety of tea viburnum with orange (rather than red) berries.

V. cassinoides bears white berries (below left) that later turn blue (below right). Some viburnums, like the *V. opulus* 'Nanum' at the left in the bottom photo, remain as low mounds and can be fit in among other plantings, such as the still-small deciduous azaleas seen here.

4

Art in the Garden

Nonhorticultural elements can certainly add distinctive and personal touches to the garden. Art can be broadly defined as an expression or application of human creative skill and imagination typically in visual form, such as a painting or sculpture, to be appreciated mainly for its beauty or emotional power. Thus, we would consider the whole garden as art (arguably the most difficult art), and inspiring imaginative creation is surely an objective of this book.

In this section, we will focus on objects, not necessarily of any great monetary value, and how we have seen them used creatively in gardens. Even very small pieces can be used in appropriate settings. This stone mythical alpine carving by Robert Keegan (left) is a surprise to be discovered among lush plantings, and a lead life-size rabbit (below left) is sited so fittingly in a lettuce patch. In contrast, the very small, unrelated figures pictured below right actually detract from an amazing collection of evergreens.

Sculptures can be major, signature features that identify a garden as distinctive to its owner. These lead eagles are innovatively placed on pedestals of varying heights in a Chestnut Hill garden. A bronze sculpture of boys in the park, by Charlotte Stokes, is a memorable addition on a brick patio in front of a thriving *Rhododendron schlippenbachii* azalea.

Children seem to be favorite features in gardens. They can add a touch of humor, as with this bronze sculpture of boys being chased up a tree by a playful dog.

Iron sheep provide an unexpected whimsical touch on an impeccably manicured lawn.

The placement of art is crucial to successfully highlighting the item and its setting, and the scale of both the piece and the plantings must be considered. *The Partners* (near right), a forged-steel sculpture by Richard Kramer, sits at the head of our driveway to symbolize the contributions both Liz and I made to our garden. In another homeowner's landscape, a life-size lead *La Brezza* (far right) luxuriates in lush surroundings.

The owners placed this bronze hippopotamus (left) adjacent to the front door as a suggestion that other unexpected delights await those who enter the garden. Below, massive, adventuresome, and most unusual figural sculptures seem to be made for their setting in the woods, while lead deer roam happily in a meadow-like area beyond a formal garden.

These bronze geese blend beautifully in appropriate scale among the rocks and ferns. Modern sculptures may be harder to integrate, but this one pictured below right appears to echo the tree seen just behind it.

Personal creative skill can help you come up with imaginative uses for natural and inexpensive materials. The owners of a Wilmington garden added an iron tongue to a nicely curved branch to make a rustic dragon. An innovative artist known as Simple used a tree in his idiosyncratic garden as a perch for one of his bird sculptures.

Putting a sculpture of a plant among live plantings is an appropriate approach, but it might have worked better to have a less busy background.

Some art pieces that you love may deserve settings designed especially for them, such as the boxwood-framed lawn around this valuable bronze boy figure by Ned Hoffman. Ivy vines (below right) build a beautiful backdrop for a bronze figure with an attractive patina.

What could be better than putting this bronze *Nude Girl with Butterfly* statue, by Rachel Marshall Hawks, adjacent to a butterfly bush (*Buddleja davidii*)? The nectar-rich flowers attract the colorful, ethereal insects.

Two other very different examples of personalizing with artistic features showcase modern touches that commemorate our garden. This weather vane, created by an artist friend, J. Donald Felix, boasts our initial and "1967," the year we started the garden. Our search for interesting features for our landscape led Liz to found Garden Accents, a company that sells garden ornaments in an elegant suburban Philadelphia showroom and online at gardenaccents.com. On a trip to Florence, Italy, we found an undiscovered source of beautiful terra cotta, and we imported the artist's pieces for Liz's business. We commissioned him to make a terra cotta jar marked with "Garden Accents" and the year the business was started, 1978. This jar (pictured below right) sits by our front door.

A rustic stone lantern in an uncommon yet readily recognized Japanese style (below left) was installed by homeowners who wanted to develop this design aesthetic in a very informal garden. The placing of garden art is certainly not easy: The antique stone Chinese figure pictured below right still hasn't found the perfect location in our garden (and seems to be exhausted by his continuing moves).

This gargoyle strikes a similar pensive pose but appears to be right at home looking out from the top of a stone wall.

Artist Barbara Chen's wonderful bronze of a happy, healthy-looking nude woman needed an important spot but not in our front yard. We settled on a site at the end of a vista on the top level of our terraced garden. A stone St. Fiacre, the patron saint of gardeners (shown below right), is ready to help in any garden setting.

This stone figure from San Agustín, Colombia, originally looked out of place isolated on an ivy-covered bank (below left) but is now better situated in a bed near a patio (below right), where it catches light in striking ways and stimulates some philosophical discussions. A type of sculpture called *el doble yo* ("the double me"), it illustrates the duality of individuals.

The owner of this small garden pool (below left) found the perfect site for Else Martinus Chapman's bronze sculpture of a boy reaching for a frog. A patch of greenery near another garden's pool (below right) is a suitable spot for a whimsical salamander. Where on earth do you think the owner found that? The same garden features a Japanese antique memorial stele situated most comfortably within dense foliage (bottom).

Consideration of scale has been important in many of the examples described in this chapter. Life-size is safest. In the photos below, the lead statue of a child seems in scale with the smaller plantings, as does this fox elevated slightly on a stump.

Sometimes sculptures larger than life-size can be used to great effect. This oversize squirrel, which welcomes visitors to a Gwynedd garden, is even more effective perched high on a stone column.

One situation in which small-scale art may work is on a wall adjacent to a patio, where you can enjoy details close-up.

5

Consider Developing Innovative Themes

A garden may have a single unifying theme that makes it distinctive or, as in our own hillside garden, takes advantage of the terrain to create a series of separate minigardens or garden rooms with a variety of themes. The following are some examples of themes that we have found effective and have seen developed in imaginative ways.

Birds

Many gardeners are interested in birds, so they may want to provide a feeder or birdbath. They may go further and truly focus on their enjoyment of birds as a theme for part of the garden. This Delaware backyard has a handmade copper-roofed, squirrelproof feeder; a collection of great birdhouses innovatively situated on a dead tree; and a bird-friendly pond.

The theme in the Delaware garden does not end with provisions for the birds. It carries through in artwork such as the bronze cranes by the pond on the previous page and the folk art birds pictured below.

A copper cupola repurposed by the same homeowners into an elegant birdhouse decorates the landscape while providing lodging for birds.

Other functional pieces with an avian theme can add idiosyncratic touches to gardens. A unique birdbath insert (below left) shows that remnants of beloved trees can certainly still be useful. A concrete birdbath (below right) displays the attractive texture that develops with aging. A small terra cotta planter (bottom) enhances another bird lover's garden wall.

Might the predatory-looking sculpture at left actually frighten away some birds? Much less threatening and more calm are a pair of lead herons that mark the ends of an arc on a mowing strip in front of an evergreen collection.

This terra cotta feeder and work of art, seen highlighted by the setting sun, is by Jean Salter. Our own bird-friendly garden has several feeders, including two for hummingbirds, and this delightful antique bronze sundial of the early bird getting the worm.

Our garden also features plants that attract birds. It's fun to choose varieties specifically for the flowers and berries that they love, such as the red fruits of this serviceberry (*Amelanchier canadensis*). Consider installing bird feeders that you can keep replenishing long after the berries are gone.

Water

Many cultures, including Chinese, Japanese, and Islamic, view water as a wonderful asset for gardens. In a fountain or stream, it can provide soothing sounds, and in a pond, such as this one at the Yu Garden in Shanghai, China, it can be a home for a collection of colorful fish or aquatic plants.

Water can also be a garden theme in various ways. If you happen to have a natural pond, it can be a welcome feature around which to build your distinctive garden and can encourage a focus on a variety of water-loving plantings.

For an alternative look, you may not even need many plants if by luck or device you have attractive rock borders and arrays of branches adding to an undisturbed natural appearance (below left). This delightful pond in Swarthmore (below right) has not only great water plants but also an eye-catching glass bubble floating among them.

Man-made pools or water features can be integrated imaginatively into a garden as well. The margin of this otherwise standard swimming pool is made more distinctive by huge rocks and an almost life-size bronze sculpture.

This Chestnut Hill garden has a more formal approach with a lead duck spraying into a circular pool from which a waterfall spills into the main pool below.

A round pool with a fountain in a quite formal garden has the surprising and humorous twist of a cute stone otter under the water spray. Another innovative gardener got both the soothing sound of a fountain and an attention-getting lead sculpture of Pan in this tiny lead pool by a patio.

This appealing bronze sculpture is situated so the girl's face is reflected in a small basin.

Small water features are effectively accented by sculptures, as shown by the accomplished gardener who nestled this little lead figure among waterside plantings.

Fountains, such as this cast-stone "teacup" at Chanticleer and a lighted patio fountain built out of a nascent stack of rocks on a slope in our garden, are captivating additions to the landscape, providing both sound and movement. If space is limited, consider a wall fountain, which offers the same sound and movement in a more compact area and can also be a work of art.

A small pool can be a focal point that draws the eye to favorite surrounding plants, like our Japanese stewartias (*Stewartia pseudocamellia*), which boast beautiful bark, and our rhododendrons. This pool, with its small waterfall, has a natural feel since it is built into a gradual slope.

Are the joys from water in the garden only achieved by human manipulation? A walk after a rain can reveal delightful details, such as the glistening beads on the needles of a limber pine (*Pinus flexilis*) or the serendipitous softening of the brick patio and bench seating with a stippling of fallen leaves.

6

Working with Colors, Textures, and Shapes

It can be fun for each of us to experiment with creative color effects and combinations in the garden. The best-laid plans can fail when the weather or unpredictable bloom timings interfere, but it's satisfying when they succeed.

Single-color themes, such as the famous white borders at Sissinghurst Castle Garden in the United Kingdom, might stimulate innovative approaches focusing on the use of one unifying color in the landscape. Some gardeners imaginatively match plant colors with garden structures, as evidenced by the red maples echoing the brick house and chair in the photos below left and center. When we saw this pink painted chair (below right) in front of a massive bed of pink summer flowers, we thought it could be interesting to repaint or switch out the chair when the planting changes.

Blue hostas echo and emphasize the tones in the patina of a bronze Buddha. Because blue tones are less common than other colors in plants, they are attention-getting in the landscape, even in garden accents such as watering cans and pots.

These gardeners successfully used a mostly monochromatic approach that features summer plantings in varying textures and shades of green.

The textures and colors of the different plants in this distinctive knot garden blend beautifully. Even sticking to a specific plant type, such as hostas (below right), can create pleasant contrasts of textures and colors that you can vary as you add new specimens.

In a Swarthmore garden (below left), green foliage in diverse textures and shapes is all that is needed beneath an overhanging Japanese maple (*Acer palmatum*). In another bed from the same garden (below right), a few flowers are integrated nicely among a variety of foliage.

When working with a group of flowering plants, it is a challenge to be sure the bloom timing does not produce unattractive plant combinations or masses of spent flowers from one variety just when another is at its glorious peak. Flowers can add temporary interesting contrasts in your groundcover textures. Scilla flowers (below left) seem to make the juniper details even more attractive. Some color combinations, such as the pink and yellow scheme displayed in the two other gardens pictured below, can be surprisingly effective.

We have loved salmon-colored flowers but have found that they are hard to integrate with other colors, so we only feature them if no plants in clashing hues are nearby. These salmon azaleas (*Rhododendron indicum* 'Macrantha') under a pine have been vigorous and bloom in June later and longer than many other azaleas. Clusters of three to five plants are generally much more effective than individual specimens. You may want to be careful when planting perennial flowering plants and be willing to move some if incompatible colors would ruin a mood you are working to achieve. On the other hand, if you want to be really idiosyncratic, you could let your garden run wild with the addition of only a few large colorful accents, as illustrated in a designer's Malvern garden (below right).

It is gratifying to search for plants whose complex flowers make color, shape, or texture combinations that are especially pleasing to you. This clerodendrum (below left) shows both its red calyxes and blue berries well into November. When we first saw the dramatic, luxuriant pinks and blues over the green foliage of *Hydrangea macrophylla* 'Tokyo Delight' (below right), we had to look for an example for our garden.

Although these lush euphorbia plants are all green, they vary dramatically in size and shape, making a distinctive and memorable display.

Combining colors, textures, and shapes that work well together takes some degree of artistic skill. The incongruous grouping below left is less appealing to the eye than the attractive combination below right, which perfectly contrasts the blues of a hosta and blue spruce with the pinks of rhododendron flowers.

Plants, of course, have distinctive shapes that we can take advantage of as we plan our gardens. Trimming or training plants can also certainly show your idiosyncracies. Some huge topiary gardens, like Ladew Gardens in Maryland or these locally famous hospital grounds in Taipei, Taiwan (below left), can be a delight to visit and perhaps inspire something you want to create when you return home. Your own plant expressions, such as training variegated ivy to drape along a wall, might be more subtle.

The shape and color of a trellis can contrast or coordinate with your plantings (below left). This glorious wisteria (below right) has been trained around a turret in a Wayne garden.

A round, trimmed sapphire berry (*Symplocos paniculata*) is an attention-getting feature in this garden (below left), while a "cloud pruned" chamaecyparis nicely borders steps leading to a sitting area in another (below right).

Many Japanese maples look distinctive and beautiful with branches left to sweep the ground like skirts, as shown below, but weeping varieties may be even more spectacular trees when pruned in layers to show their graceful branching.

Prime chances for blending colors and shapes are not limited to the spring or summer. Here the rich orange red of a sourwood (*Oxydendrum arboreum*), burgundy of a tall stewartia (*Stewartia monadelpha*), and orange yellow of a Japanese maple in fall contrast with the yellow foliage of the trees in the background.

Rocks can also contribute unique shapes and textures among your plants and may occasionally be independent focal points. If you are lucky (and/or imaginative), you may unearth something potentially interesting during your preparation of holes for plantings, as we did when we dug up the trio of rocks shown below. They look sculptural in our garden with plantings in summer or snow in winter. In another garden (bottom), rocks were arranged to suggest an almost mythical scene. If you unearth no rocks with which to experiment, you may want to go to a local quarry in search of a specific size, shape, or color. Some rocks can serve practical purposes as seats, stairs, borders, or stepping stones.

A dramatically pockmarked rock was already a unique accent in a planting but became even more intriguing when a tiny volunteer seedling made a home in a dirt-filled crevice. A red-brown igneous rock seems a fine companion for heather.

Stacks of rocks called cairns have long been traditional among native peoples in North America. These may have ceremonial implications or may simply be trail markers, and they are most commonly found in barren areas. Below left is an interpretation of a cairn in a suburban Philadelphia garden, where other scattered stones were used as a border. Perhaps you have some local stones to make your own distinctive cairn. A collection of shaped rocks (below right) includes a cairn-like pile.

After seeing dramatic 4-foot-diameter rock spheres in a pre-Columbian site in Costa Rica, we added similar granite spheres in groups or as isolated accents in an expanse of pachysandra (below left). A similar but smaller stone ball (below right) works quite well next to European wild ginger (*Asarum europaeum*) and other thriving plantings.

Natural rocks in the landscape can provide wonderful contrasts for plantings and even become props for fanciful displays.

This round, textured rock serves as a base for an abstract snake-like figure.

Paths and steps are more traditional uses for rocks and stones. Rough-hewn stones work well in an informal set of steps, while flat and irregular rocks arranged in a circular pattern can form a natural seating alcove.

As we emphasized in our discussion of water features, impressive rocks like these can both provide a streambed and define its borders.

In a design by Hiroshi Makita, huge rocks form the structure for a dramatic waterfall and contrast with the plantings.

Collecting rocks can be fun and intellectually stimulating for gardeners, but can their collections be overdone, adding little aesthetically to the garden? Yes.

Lines—straight or curved, horizontal or vertical—can add structure, character, and personality and offer gardeners plenty of room for creativity. This trimmed yew hedge along the street (below left) separates a rhododendron woods situated beyond and provides the pattern for a linear bed to embellish the view of a large residence. In the garden below right, trees are being trimmed so that the trunks are parallel to vertical elements in the home and the foliage is parallel to the horizontal flowerbed.

The straight lines of a path or planting can lead to a focal point or an exit.

A series of vertical posts helps accent a set of horizontal steps (below left). We love this cluster of vertical katsura trunks (below right) that creates a protected spot for sitting or could be imagined as a site for a secluded shrine.

Gardeners tend to favor curved lines over straight, and guidelines are available to help them design attractive curves. Curved paths can vary from a traditional, elegant entry walkway (below left) to a more casual trail that subtly slows your pace to encourage the viewing of special plantings, such as this dwarf evergreen garden (below right).

A curved wooden bridge uses angles reminiscent of those in traditional Asian gardens.

Vertical lines from tree trunks suggested a spot in this Swarthmore garden for a vertical sculpture. In another garden, a horizontal wall all but beckoned this reclining figure.

A strong horizontal branch must have been irresistible to this ivy that tracked along it. But strong lines creating interest are not always parallel, as shown by the beautiful twisted branches of a beech tree in winter.

Developing Focal Points

The focal points that you select emphasize your personal style preferences and interests. They lead the eye through the garden or enhance the garden's view from key spots, including from inside your home in winter. Perhaps the classic idea of a focal point would be a temple-like enclosure over a fountain at the end of a grassy walkway. The example shown at left adds to the formal feel of this garden.

For many gardens, the perfect focal point is a prized plant, such as this old, wonderfully gnarled weeping cherry located at the branching of a brick path (above right).

A prized specimen tree may also punctuate the end of a broad lawn. The skillfully pruned euonymus at right leads the eye up to its great shape but also down to the sculptures in this bird-themed garden.

This unusual specimen katsura (below left) was used by the proud owner to lead from a lawn toward a covered pathway. Focal points may change with the seasons. A serviceberry (below right) attracts attention to itself and the nearby imaginative rock arrangement most effectively when it is flowering.

You can further accentuate an intended focal point by enhancing the setting. This Haverford pool and subtle fountain with its pleasing sound is a more important destination thanks to the strong semicircle of evergreens and urns around it.

Favorite nonhorticultural acquisitions, such as the antique iron urn pictured at left, can highlight a beautiful planting or floral display.

In our own eclectic terraced garden, we have added a series of focal points to direct visitors and keep their interest. One example is this antique stone Aztec warrior purchased in a pawn shop in Mexico City's Zócalo. It leads the eye up a flight of steps, not only to the sculpture but also to the surrounding leucothoe, which is attractive even in March.

Your most important focal points may be at sites that you can see year-round from inside the house. Both our bedroom and kitchen look out on a bank where we sited this *Cercis canadensis* var. *texensis* 'Traveller', which has special meaning for Liz because her mother both lived in Texas and traveled widely. While this is glorious in bloom, its weeping branches are also attractive in winter and can be decorated seasonally with Easter eggs, Christmas lights, or other ornaments meaningful to your family.

We sited a bronze sculpture partially up this hillside to lead the eye (and guests) up the series of steps to three levels: the stroll garden, the croquet lawn, and the upper terrace.

A sundial could help impart a traditional ambience, but this setting is still a work in progress.

This site at the end of a grassy path is crying out for a reasonably large-scale focal point.

How about creating a focal point with several components? Here a bed containing a paperbark cherry (*Prunus serrula*), a large igneous rock, bulbs, a rhododendron, and a small but important Japanese memorial stele steers one's focus across the lawn to a set of steps.

8

Take Advantage of Changes with the Seasons

We have embraced the challenging and interesting opportunity to choose plantings, designs, and features that have created attractive and distinctive views of our garden in all seasons. We hope you can delight in many of the variations that take place in your own landscape as the seasons change. Think especially about views that you see from various rooms in your home. Winter in northern climes can offer a wonderful chance for enjoying more depth and details not seen in summer, as deciduous plants lose their foliage. Note how the terraced slope behind our home is opened up in winter and structural components become more prominent, particularly when accented by snow.

This charming bird sculpture in a Wilmington garden (below left) is virtually invisible in summer but becomes a great accent on the bare branches in winter. Another way to make a garden distinctive is to focus on barks that add all-year interest with their colors, textures, or sculptural shapes such as the gnarled form of this Harry Lauder's walking stick (*Corylus avellana* 'Contorta'), pictured below right.

We specifically chose to collect and plant a number of trees with decorative bark so that they could be seen from our glass-walled bedroom and plant room. They are of interest all year but especially in fall and winter. The maackia (*Maackia amurensis*) pictured below left and center features both interesting bark and fall color. *Lagerstroemia* 'Natchez' crape myrtle (below right) and lacebark pine (*Pinus bungeana*) and paperbark maple (*Acer griseum*), shown bottom left and right respectively, are some of the other trees we have enjoyed.

The maackia is magical when coated with ice, as seen in this view from our cozy bedroom. Our coral bark Japanese maple (*Acer palmatum* 'Sango-kaku'), with its dramatic red bark, is another true winter pleasure.

It's a visual treat when ice glistens on that red bark and decorates our bedroom window.

Some of our trees with winter interest are out in front of our home, and we enjoy seeing them as we come and go. Three river birches, including *Betula nigra* 'Cully' (trade name Heritage), pictured below left, and a huge, multistemmed Persian ironwood (*Parrotia persica*), not pictured, feature attractive bark that looks beautiful year-round. Further up the hillside but easily viewed on a clear winter day is a paperbark cherry, shown below right with peeling red bark shining in the December sun.

Berries also create exceptional winter interest. This crabapple, with its bright-red fruits highlighted against the blue winter sky, is another seasonal treat.

Of course, trees with attractive bark may have other desirable special features. One example is the Franklin tree (*Franklinia alatamaha*). Philadelphia-area residents may want to show pride in our famous 18th-century plant explorer, John Bartram, by growing this tree, which Bartram found in North Carolina—where it no longer grows in the wild—and named after his friend (and notorious gout sufferer) Benjamin Franklin. The beautiful white flowers appearing late in the summer are always a conversation piece, as is the lovely bark, shown below with spring hostas and tulips and, in another garden, with summer foliage.

Well-positioned garden ornaments can be effective at emphasizing your interests in all seasons. Here an antique Japanese lantern is seen adjacent to the steps of a garden path in summer and in winter.

Our stone Aztec warrior unfortunately does not look nearly as comfortable in the winter snow as he does next to the fall color of the oakleaf hydrangea (*Hydrangea quercifolia*).

We have sometimes lamented the curled leaves of our rhododendrons in winter, but the beautiful full buds are harbingers of spring.

In late winter or very early spring, you can begin to see some changes in the garden if you have planned well. We have gradually focused on a variety of yellow-flowering plants that show up in the beginning of March. All can be seen from inside our home and on our early outdoor explorations close to the house. A witch hazel (*Hamamelis*) blooms first, and its blossoms are sometimes adorned with snow.

The witch hazel flowers are closely followed by those of a cornelian cherry dogwood (*Cornus mas*).

Those two early-blooming plants are near the patio, where they are seen from the bedroom and plant room. We have a lovely pale-yellow winter hazel (*Corylopsis pauciflora*) visible from the living room window, forsythias lining the driveway, and wonderful yellow daffodils in a bed outside the kitchen and in several sweeps up the hillside behind the house. Slightly later in April, *Kerria japonica* 'Simplex' (a Japanese kerria with rich-yellow flowers) blooms on the same hillside. The cheery flowers, shown below left, stand out among the pale-green new growth of the kerria's leaves. While yellow is an easy choice for early color in many gardens, you could certainly try the pinks from cherries or rhododendrons, such as the PJM Group rhododendron pictured below right.

Even before azaleas flower, their buds look pretty when accented by an early-spring snow. Many early-flowering plants are especially dramatic since the blooms form on bare branches. This April-flowering dwarf fothergilla (*Fothergilla gardenii*) is one enjoyable example.

Most gardeners are well aware of the potential design effects plants and trees can bring to the garden in autumn, when foliage colors are on brilliant display. But how can you take that potential to an idiosyncratic level?

Think about how you might use plants with great fall color in distinctive ways that have special meaning for you. For example, we placed this oakleaf hydrangea in a prominent position near a woods so we could enjoy it as we do fall cleanups.

Too often people base the siting of plants on the sexy spring flowers they like to show off. It's fun to try to develop settings where fall colors create a memorable image, such as this scene where Japanese stewartia trees seem to shelter the Chinese stone figures.

The scarlet leaves of redvein enkianthus (*Enkianthus campanulatus*) and the yellow heart-shaped foliage of the katsura provide outstanding color next to and above our patio in autumn. In our area, we eagerly anticipate the katsura's fall color, because in some years it has been distinctly more orange, as shown in the photo below right.

The bright-red Virginia creeper (*Parthenocissus quinquefolia*) invading the English ivy (*Hedera helix*) was initially an undesirable surprise in this garden, but in subsequent autumns it was embraced as a welcome pop of color.

It is important to intentionally notice and fully appreciate the predictable beauty of the fall transformation of Japanese maple trees.

Some flowers can still accent the fall garden. One predictable example is autumn crocus (*Colchicum autumnale*), pictured below amid spiky iris leaves and vinca groundcover. The source of colchicine, a traditional drug prescribed for gout, this plant is an obvious choice for the garden of a doctor who has done research on and treated people with this inflammatory condition. Autumn crocus has luxuriant spring foliage that can almost be lost among the irises, which help to disguise the crocus leaves as they fade and become rather unsightly. When the beautiful lavender-pink flowers appear in fall, it's amusing to test visiting doctors on what they may be.

Obviously we can't discuss seasons without referring to both spring and summer, which are covered in more detail as we discuss other gardening aspects throughout the book, but here are a few examples of some special effects. These crocuses (below left) seem especially delightful under the sculpted bare branches of a Japanese maple in early April, and azaleas and rhododendrons (below right) are picture-perfect complements to a paperbark maple in May.

One caution about luxuriously flowering spring trees like this Japanese snowbell (*Styrax japonicus*): When flower seeds fall on receptive mulch, they may well germinate and require extremely labor-intensive weeding.

9

What Can Planters Add?

As long as you can make a drainage hole, any container, no matter how quirky, can be used as a planter by the adventuresome gardener who wants to add distinctive features. This old stone washbasin (left) works well as a planter in its setting, as do a pair of bronze Mindanao sword holders (below), which not only look unique but also have plenty of openings that provide good drainage. A fairly simple or neutral container can be planted with virtually anything of appropriate size.

An old, eviscerated piano is so eye-catching that simple flowering annuals are all that it needs to make an effective announcement. If you are inclined to load a planter with a really exuberant collection (as shown below right), the type of container may not even matter.

Planting in an overturned terra cotta vessel can add a different twist, and this is also a good way to use broken or chipped planters. Simple planters like the one shown on a circle of Belgian blocks can be nicely set off by their surroundings. This design would look even better if the planter were larger.

Vessels such as terra cotta storage jars and an antique French container can be attractive whether they are empty or used to showcase plants.

At a shop in Philadelphia's Chinatown, we found some containers used to ship "thousand-year-old eggs," and we have used them as planters and as more purely decorative features. One is being used here as a small table between two seats on the patio. Remember, if you have a colorful, decorated planter, such as the floral pot below, it may look too busy if heavily planted with clashing flowers. An old, weathered planter with encroaching moss is a lovely complement to cheery blooms and also creates a feeling that an area has been long established and is well settled.

You may have fun making your own hypertufa planter with Portland cement, perlite, and peat moss. You can customize the shape, size, and, if you add pigment to the cement, color.

How about considering walls and gaps in paving stones as planters? These stepping stones and stone steps provide welcoming niches for plantings that soften the appearance of the stonework.

Planting on a wall in some soil between the rocks or in attached iron or terra cotta pots can be a wonderful way to display your favorite plants.

Even our most inspired idiosyncratic gardener should not forget practicality when using planters. Some containers that are made of heavy, fragile materials or hold tender plants may have to be moved indoors for the winter. These wheeled platforms could make that process easier and prevent some painful back injuries.

Structures in the Garden

A variety of modest to ambitious structural additions to a garden can be practical, extremely idiosyncratic, or both. Not everything can be as impressive as this pergola surrounded by luxurious plantings at the Chelsea Flower Show in London.

The tree house pictured below left fits beautifully in its woodland setting and could be a place for imaginative adventures for children and periodic respites for grownups. At the end of a lawn in a Haverford garden (below right) sits a structure that could function as a disguised storage space, but isn't its use as a children's play area or owner's getaway much more fun?

This certainly idiosyncratic garden has a model mansion among the inexpensive painted ornaments at a mountain vacation home.

Liz designed our own Japanese-style "teahouse" to help create a peaceful, calm mood and provide a place to relax, take in the view, and enjoy an occasional meal. The structure, with its moon window, was inspired by memories of childhood days in Japan, where she lived next door to the Meiji Shrine. An Asian influence has clearly guided the personalization of our garden.

Lathhouses can be used to display collections of shade-loving plants, such as orchids, during the summer. Consider how similar structures might be used to express your original approaches.

Wood structures can add beauty and function to garden spaces, as shown by this composting bin (below left), built by Liz's father; a rose trellis (below center), constructed by a Collegeville gardener; and elevated beds carefully prepared for a wheelchair gardener.

Birds have enjoyed this attention-getting arch, crafted with a series of cedar birdhouses and extending over a path toward another compost area on our property, almost as much as we have. Unfortunately, squirrels love to nibble on it too.

This more imposing arch on an estate (below left) is enhanced by a simple iron gate that opens to a broad lawn. In the unique gate pictured below right, the owners inserted an ornate piece of antique ironwork.

We had this decorative iron gate made to insert into a simple iron fence built for the very practical purpose of excluding deer from the garden.

Some properties in our area contain structures designed specifically for a space, such as this stone bridge over a pebble "sea," which was created by Hiroshi Makita for a Japanese garden. Other properties boast structures that have been redesigned to serve a new purpose, such as this old springhouse that was turned into a pool house. Perhaps you might be able to repurpose an existing structure to beautify and improve your landscape.

11

Delight in the Transient Moments

  When we work in the garden or just wander around to enjoy it, we often stumble upon serendipitous scenes. We had appropriately planted a Japanese maple behind our cedar Japanese-style teahouse but were especially delighted one spring to see the wooden roof as a canvas decorated with a subtle display of the maple's flowers. In autumn, the roof was "painted" with its fallen leaves.

A similar stippling of cherry blossoms on junipers and a Chinese stone sculpture was a very transient pleasure one spring. The pink blossoms remaining on the trees looked dramatic against a vividly blue sky.

Plants that pop up as volunteers in unexpected spots can be temporary delights. A Japanese snowbell had been unusually prolific in dropping seeds, which germinated like weeds in our garden. Even years after we moved the snowbell to a new location, we would find seedlings of this species looking quite healthy and transiently nice among the junipers at the plant's original site (below left). We had similar adventures with crown vetch that we had used as an early groundcover to stabilize our hillside. It did the job but began to overgrow everything else (below right).

Despite many years of digging and trying to get all the roots, the vetch kept reappearing. This completely frustrated us and reminded us that not every unexpected development is a delight. After a long vacation, this overgrown path that required cleaning up showed us how gardening is really a difficult and demanding art and that garden spaces require regular attention.

This rainbow in the spray of a sprinkler was a pleasing momentary delight, even though problems with our lawn had necessitated its watering.

We are always amazed by the beauty of the pale-green new growth on some rhododendrons, and it can easily be missed if you don't explore the garden regularly. We hope you are able to get out in the garden to wander—and not just when there is work to do. After one rainy spell, we were surprised by these mushrooms emerging from the wood-chip mulch.

We also noticed these toadstools in a path. And this beautifully crafted spiderweb was found early one morning and was gone a few hours later.

An occasional serendipitous image can only be appreciated after the fact. This photo of the azaleas outside our plant room shows a reflection of me taking the picture. As mentioned previously, nowhere near all transient moments are as attractive or as fleeting as we might wish. Rather unsightly piles of wood chips and mulch have been frequent additions to our driveway.

The petunias in this bed, which had been cultivated by our daughter Heidi, were disappointingly transient because her interest in the horticultural adventure turned out to be transient as well.

12

A Garden Is for People

A garden is perhaps best personalized by the presence of both the people who built and maintain it and the friends who enjoy sharing in it. Welcoming access points, clear, easy-to-navigate paths, and especially well-situated places for sitting, resting, gazing, or discussing can be key to peopling the garden. The hammock in the top photo was placed under a kousa dogwood (*Cornus kousa*) so one could recline in thought while looking across the garden. We positioned our own shaded hammock (pictured in the bottom photo) in a perfect location for relaxing or viewing heated croquet matches on the adjacent broad lawn.

Consider developing a relatively isolated space for contemplation. Many of the earliest medieval gardens had such sanctuaries. Wouldn't this still be an attractive feature? Let your imagination go when picking seats and the spots where you'll scatter them around. The very original white-and-gray chair pictured below sits in a Wilmington garden. The antique French spring steel chairs are much more comfortable than they might appear and need no cushions. It can be fun to search for these antique chairs, which are quite distinctive but unfortunately hard to find.

A heavy, durable material such as teak can be a practical choice for garden furniture. While a teak bench is an inviting summer stop, it is sturdy enough to be left out (as a very cold seat) in the winter. For years, we had further personalized this area with variegated bishop's goutweed (*Aegopodium podagraria* 'Variegatum'), which is pictured in the springtime photo at the bottom right. This planting was inspired by my research on gout and my specialty of rheumatology.

Some gardens being restored on old estates would originally have had permanent seating like the stone bench pictured below.

Scent can be a compelling pleasure in the garden, whether fragrant plants are sited near where people sit or in out-of-the-way places where an encounter with their aroma might surprise and delight.

Japanese clethra (*Clethra barbinervis*), pictured below left, has fragrant flowers that last late into the summer. The white, sweetly fragrant flowers of thorny olive (*Elaeagnus pungens*), shown below right, appear in late October. One would not expect such a pleasant fragrance from a plant with the name *pungens*. This specimen, which is located next to our patio, needs some pruning to keep it in scale.

Two other plants on our property feature fragrances we enjoy. The katsura's falling autumn leaves have a delicious cotton candy scent. The huge, white, fragrant blossoms of moonflower (*Ipomoea alba*) open only in the evening. You might consider lighting areas of the garden that may be best appreciated at night.

Foul-smelling plants attract a totally different kind of attention and should be placed off the beaten track. We originally located a dragon arum (*Dracunculus vulgaris*) next to the path to our patio for its dramatic—albeit phallic—flower. It received lots of recognition on tours of our garden, but we eventually removed the plant because the bloom's odor of decaying flesh, which effectively entices pollinators, was truly awful.

In addition to welcoming visitors into our own garden, Liz and I have thoroughly enjoyed visiting other gardens to appreciate what fellow gardeners have created and to look for new inspiration. I took many of the photographs that illustrate the concepts in this book on Philadelphia-area garden tours. In the top photo, Liz is pictured on one such tour organized by the Pennsylvania Horticultural Society. The group image is from a series of tours that I organized and conducted to raise money for arthritis research at the University of Pennsylvania.

Conclusion

Nowhere near all innovations are successful, and even the most effective plantings can become out of scale, intolerant of changing amounts of shade, or unattractive from disease or storm damage. Damage by deer has been a relatively recent problem in our area. The pictured rhododendron was decimated by them despite our using recommended deterrents such as soap and even some lion urine from the zoo. It is critical to be willing to change. Think of change as a fun opportunity to try a new approach. Might that approach be to simplify by not replacing everything? Empty space can sometimes open up surprising and pleasing views. Gardening is a most difficult and constantly evolving form of art, but it's one that is rewarding and encourages so many ways to innovate and to be idiosyncratic.

About the Authors

The authors began gardening together in 1967 and in the ensuing years created an award-winning terraced hillside garden in Gulph Mills, Pennsylvania. They have written about their garden in various publications and opened it for many groups as it evolved. In 2015, it was recognized by inclusion in the Smithsonian Institution's Archives of American Gardens.

H. Ralph Schumacher was a pioneering rheumatologist, researcher, and professor of medicine at the University of Pennsylvania, and he was also an avid gardener. He operated a series of garden tours in the Philadelphia area from 1987 through 1993 to support arthritis research. During these tours, he photographed the innovative garden features that became the basis for this book. As a rheumatologist, he lectured all around the world, always keeping his eyes peeled for treasures that could be sold at Garden Accents, a showroom of garden art and accessories that his wife, Elizabeth "Liz" S. Schumacher, founded in 1978. He thoroughly enjoyed his side hustle as a "buyer" for Garden Accents.

Liz graduated from the Barnes Foundation horticulture program the same year she started Garden Accents, a business built on her experience with developing and accenting the family garden with distinctive features from her and Ralph's travels and other sources. For this showroom (accessible online at gardenaccents.com), she has collected an assortment of original items available only at Garden Accents. For sale are more than 5,000 garden pieces, including fountains, planters, sculptures, outdoor furniture, and unique accessories. Liz has lectured widely on art in the garden and how to create and personalize memorable gardens.

Printed in the United States
by Baker & Taylor Publisher Services